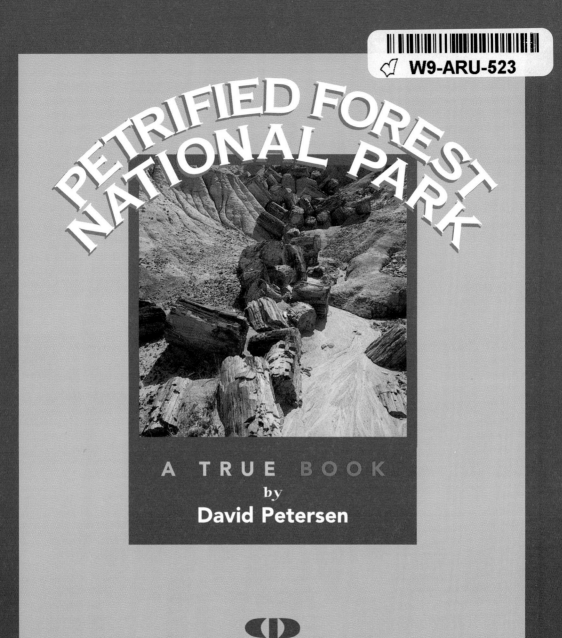

PETRIFIED FOREST NATIONAL PARK

A TRUE BOOK

by
David Petersen

Children's Press®
A Division of Grolier Publishing

New York London Hong Kong Sydney
Danbury, Connecticut

For Ben Abbey

Reading Consultant
Linda Cornwell
Learning Resource Consultant
Indiana Department of
Education

Petrified Forest National
Park contains more petrified
wood than anywhere else in
the world.

Library of Congress Cataloging-in-Publication Data

Petersen, David, 1946-
    Petrified Forest National Park / by David Petersen.
        p.   cm. — (A true book)
    Includes index.
    Summary: Describes the geological history, sights, and facilities of
Arizona's Petrified Forest National Park.
    ISBN 0-516-20052-6 (lib. bdg.)   ISBN 0-516-26111-8 (pbk.)
    1. Petrified Forest National Park (Ariz.)—Juvenile literature.
[1. Petrified Forest National Park (Ariz.) 2. National parks and reserves.]
I. Title. II. Series.
F817.P4P45   1996
979.1'37—dc20   96-1181
                                                                   CIP
                                                                    AC

Contents

Petrified Forest National Park

Have you ever heard of a forest with trees made of stone? Would you like to see one?

You can, because such a place really exists. It's called Petrified Forest National Park, and it's located in northern Arizona.

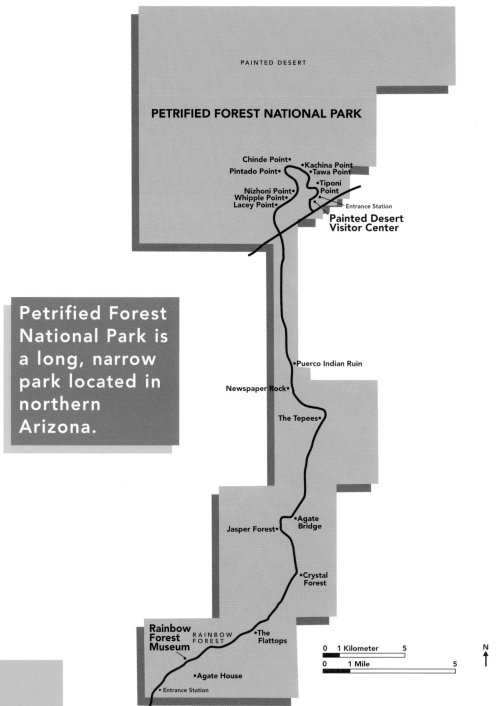

PAINTED DESERT

PETRIFIED FOREST NATIONAL PARK

Chinde Point•
Pintado Point•   •Kachina Point
              •Tawa Point
              •Tiponi
              Point
Nizhoni Point•
Whipple Point•
Lacey Point•   •Entrance Station

**Painted Desert
Visitor Center**

Petrified Forest
National Park is
a long, narrow
park located in
northern
Arizona.

•Puerco Indian Ruin

Newspaper Rock•

The Tepees•

                    •Agate
                    Bridge
Jasper Forest•

                    •Crystal
                    Forest

**Rainbow
Forest
Museum**   RAINBOW
            FOREST   •The
                      Flattops

                    0   1 Kilometer   5

                    0   1 Mile   5

•Agate House

• Entrance Station

N
↑

6

These petrified logs have been here for thousands of years.

There, you'll see rainbow-colored stone columns where green, living trees once stood. The word petrified means "turned to stone."

Petrified Forest also has stone animals—the fossils of huge reptiles and amphibians that lived long ago, even before the dinosaurs. Fossils are the stone remains of animals and plants.

How long ago did these petrified trees and fossilized animals live? Try to imagine a time called the Triassic Period, 225 million years ago.

Today, the Petrified Forest is a hot, dry desert, but back

Skeletons of the dinosaurs that roamed the area 225 million years ago are displayed at the park's museums (above). Also on display are the fossilized remains of ancient plants (left).

then, it was green and wet with lots of streams and marshes. Thick forests of giant pine-like trees stood 250 feet (76 meters) high! Strange amphibians and reptiles lived in the water and on the land.

These were the trees and animals that we see today, preserved in stone. How could this happen? How could living things be turned to stone?

How Petrification Works

As the trees died, they were washed away by streams that carried them into huge marshes. When the trees sank to the bottom of the marshes, they were covered with sediment.

Meanwhile, nearby volcanoes often erupted, spewing

tons of volcanic ash into the air. As the ash fell back to earth, it was washed into the marsh. The ash dissolved in the marsh water, soaking down through the sediment and into the buried trees.

Volcanic ash contains a mineral called silica. As the wood of the trees rotted away, it was replaced by silica absorbed from the water. When the marsh dried up, the silica hardened into a glass-like stone called quartz.

Small pieces of petrified wood
are found throughout the park.

The trees didn't really turn to stone. Their wood was just replaced by stone. The stone trees are so perfect that you can see the grain of the wood, the knot-holes, and even the trees' growth rings.

Other minerals in the marsh water—such as carbon, iron, and manganese—gave the petrified wood its beautiful colors. Reds, blues, browns, greens, yellows—all these colors can be found on the stone trees of Petrified Forest.

A cross-section of a petrified log (left), shows the tree's growth rings. Many colors can be seen in just one piece of petrified wood (right).

Fossils

For millions of years, the buried trees lay beneath the ancient marsh sediment. These deposits grew thicker and thicker until the logs were buried 1,500 feet (457 m) deep.

Meanwhile, many marsh animals died, became buried in the sediment, and slowly fossilized—just like the trees.

Animal fossils of the Petrified Forest include insects, snails, clams, crabs, fish, amphibians, reptiles, and dinosaurs.

One of the biggest fossilized animals found in Petrified Forest is the Phytosaur. This monster looked like a giant crocodile with huge, snaggly teeth and grew up to 30 feet long (9 m).

Its fossilized bones can be seen at the park's two museums.

But how did the buried stone animals and trees get to the earth's surface where they are found today?

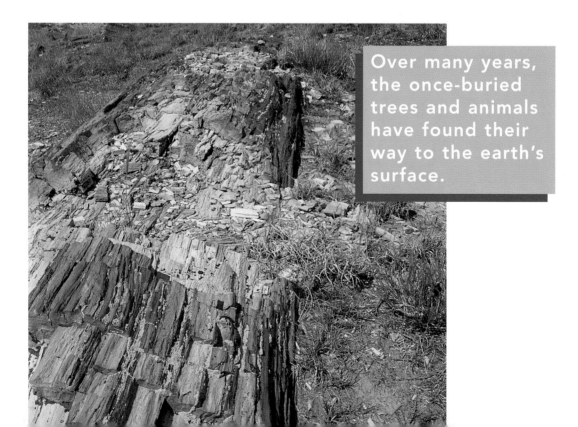

Over many years, the once-buried trees and animals have found their way to the earth's surface.

Geology Takes Over

About 60 million years ago, pressure inside the earth caused the land containing Petrified Forest to bulge upward, forming hills of sandstone, siltstone, mudstone, and clay. Within these hills, which had once been the floor of the marsh, lay thousands of petrified trees and fossils.

Tremendous pressure inside the earth forced these logs upward to the surface.

Then erosion began to eat away at the exposed hills. Rain, snow, and ice—the principal elements of erosion—broke the soft stone into individual grains. Wind and water carried away the grains of rock.

As the hills were worn away, hundreds of stone logs and animal fossils were exposed. No one knows how many more are still buried. Then, more than 2,000 years ago, humans wandered into this magical landscape.

Visitors enjoy exploring the Painted Desert region of Petrified Forest National Park.

Anasazi— The Ancient Ones

The first people to see the Petrified Forest were prehistoric American Indians. They were probably hunters following herds of wild animals. All that remains of these early people are a few stone tools, such as arrowheads, axes, and hammers.

Navajo Indians who live near the park today call these mysterious ancient people the Anasazi, which means "the Ancient Ones."

Gradually, the Anasazi learned how to farm. They also learned how to build strong houses of stone. Several

Puerco Ruins is the best example of an Anasazi pueblo found in the park.

Anasazi houses were joined together to make a pueblo, or village.

Puerco Ruins is the finest example of an Anasazi pueblo in Petrified Forest. Built about 900 years ago, it had 75 rooms and housed 60 to 70 people. Only the stone walls of the ancient pueblo remain standing today. But just below the pueblo ruins, you can see the Puerco art gallery. Pecked into the surfaces of dark-stained sandstone boulders are dozens of Anasazi rock carvings called petroglyphs. These engravings show people, animals, and mysterious symbols no one understands. There are more petroglyphs at nearby Newspaper Rock.

Petroglyphs, ancient Anasazi rock carvings, can be seen at the Puerco art gallery. The meaning of the Anasazi's symbols and carvings remains a mystery.

Sometimes, the Anasazi used petrified wood to build their houses. The best preserved of these dwellings is Agate House—the oldest wood house in the world!

About 600 years ago, the Anasazi left Petrified Forest for areas with more water. Today's Hopi Indians of Arizona and New Mexico believe they are descendants of the Ancient Ones.

Agate House is the oldest wood house in the world.

Anasazi Ruins

In addition to Petrified Forest National Park, Anasazi ruins can be found in many areas of the southwestern United States.

Mesa Verde National Park in Colorado contains an Anasazi site called the Cliff Palace. Mesa Verde also has ruins called Spruce Tree House, Square Tower House, and Sun Temple.

Chaco Culture National Historical Park in New Mexico has the ruins of thirteen Anasazi dwellings. The best-known is called Pueblo Bonito, a four-story, 800-room building.

Anasazi ruins can also be seen at Aztec Ruins National Monument, New Mexico; Canyon de Chelly National Monument, Arizona; and Walnut Canyon National Monument, also in Arizona.

A Foreign Culture Invades

During the 1500s, Spanish explorers were the first Europeans to see the stone trees. But Petrified Forest did not become well known until the mid-1800s.

The Spanish were followed by people who were surveyors

and mapmakers. Soon ranchers, farmers, and a few hardy tourists came. Some of these people discovered they could collect and sell the petrified wood. A few of them even used dynamite to blow the logs apart, hoping to find valuable crystals inside. Clearly, something had to be done to protect this special place.

Finally, in 1906, President Theodore Roosevelt made Petrified Forest a national monument.

Greedy people would no longer
be able to plunder the treasure
of stone trees for profit. In 1962,
Petrified Forest became a
national park.

Petrified Forest became a
national park in 1962.

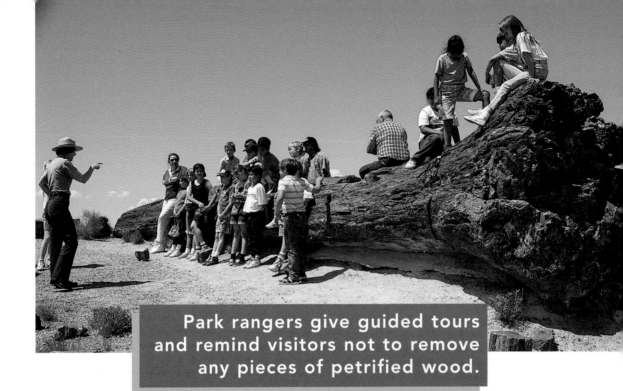

Park rangers give guided tours and remind visitors not to remove any pieces of petrified wood.

Today, the trees, fossils, Indian ruins, and a corner of the Painted Desert are protected for all people to enjoy for all time. You can help by leaving things as you found them. Don't take anything away when you visit.

A Tour Of Petrified Forest

Petrified Forest National Park is long and narrow. A 27-mile-long (43-kilometers) road runs through the middle of the park. Many scenic view points lie along this road, and short foot trails lead you to special hidden places.

Displays at the park museums explain how the ancient trees became petrified.

If you enter the park from the north entrance, stop first at the Painted Desert Visitor Center. At the museum there, you'll see displays of petrified wood and fossils. Take a few minutes to watch the film explaining how the ancient trees were petrified.

Along a big curve in the park road just north of the museum

are eight scenic points. Each one—Tiponi, Tawa, Kachina, Chinde, Pintado, Nizhoni, Whipple, and Lacey—offers a beautiful view of the park's 43,020-acre (17,409-hectare) Painted Desert Wilderness.

Painted Desert Wilderness, as seen from Lacey Point

The road runs straight south to Puerco Ruins. Spend some time exploring this Anasazi village and its fascinating rock art.

Next comes Newspaper Rock. Depending on light conditions, you may have to squint to see the American Indian art on the black boulders below the viewing area. But it's there—hundreds of petroglyphs!

A little farther south are The Tepees—big, pointed, striped hills of dark clay, light sandstone, and reddish siltstone.

The Tepees of
Petrified Forest

Agate Bridge was accidently formed millions of years ago.

At Agate Bridge, a petrified log lies across a ravine, forming a natural bridge. But don't try to walk on it! It's millions of years old and could collapse at any time.

At Jasper and Crystal forests you can wander around among hundreds of petrified logs. Try to imagine this place as a huge forest 225 million years ago.

Visitors examine the petrified logs of Crystal Forest.

Boulders near the Flattops parking area.

Then, from the Flattops parking area, you can hike into the park's second wilderness area—the 7,240-acre (2,930-hectare) Rainbow Forest. Just before reaching the Rainbow Forest Museum at the south end of the park,

is the short hiking trail to
Agate House.

All along the way, watch for
wildlife. The park's largest animal is the pronghorn antelope,
but you're more likely to see
rabbits, snakes, lizards, ravens,
and other small creatures.

The pronghorn antelope is the park's largest inhabitant.

Petrified Forest National Park is a
fun and interesting place to visit.

Now you've seen Petrified
Forest National Park—the
place where history is written
in stone.

Junior Ranger

While you're at the Rainbow Forest Museum, be sure to ask one of the park rangers there about the Junior Ranger program. The program is interesting, educational, and fun. And the Junior Ranger patch you will earn after completing the program will be yours to keep!

This Certifies That

_____

has completed the Junior Ranger Program at

PETRIFIED FOREST NATIONAL PARK

and is hereby considered an official

JUNIOR RANGER

Given on the _____ day of _____, 19___

_____
Ranger

To Find Out More

Here are some additional resources to help you learn more about Petrified Forest National Park.

 **Books**

Brown, Richard. **A Kid's Guide to National Parks.** Harcourt Brace, 1989.

Diamond, Lynnell. **Let's Discover Petrified Forest National Park: A Children's Activity Book for Ages 6-11**. Mountaineers, 1991.

Fradin, Dennis. **Arizona.** Children's Press, 1993.

Mead, Robin, et al. **Our National Parks.** Smithmark, 1993.

 **Organizations**

Petrified Forest National Park
Painted Desert Visitor Center
Petrified Forest National Park, AZ 86028

National Park Service
Office of Public Inquiries
P.O. Box 37127
Washington, DC 20013
202-208-4747

Western Region
National Park Service
600 Harrison Street
Suite 600
San Francisco, CA 94107

National Parks and Conservation Association
1776 Massachusetts
  Avenue, NW
Washington, DC 20036
800-NAT-PARK
natparks@aol.com
npca@npca.org

Great Outdoor Recreation Pages (GORP)
http://www.gorp.com/gorp/ resource/US_National_Park/ main.htm

Information on hiking, fishing, boating, climate, places to stay, plant life, wildlife, and more.

National Park Foundation
CompuServe offers online maps, park products, special programs, a question-and-answer series, and in-depth information available by park name, state, region, or interest. From the main menu, select *Travel,* then *Where To Go,* then *Complete Guide to America's National Parks.*

National Park Service World Wide Web Server
http://www.nps.gov

Includes virtual tours, maps, and essays.

National Parks Magazine
editorial@npca.org

Focuses on the park system in general, as well as on individual sites.

Note: Many of the national parks have their own home pages on the World Wide Web. Do some exploring!

Important Words

amphibian animal that lives part of its life in water and part on land; frogs, toads, and salamanders are amphibians

geology the study of the Earth and its features

gully small valley

ravine very narrow valley usually formed by erosion

reptile animal—such as a snake, lizard, or turtle—that crawls, or moves, on its belly

sediment tiny particles (usually silt, sand, and clay) that are dissolved in water, then settle in layers

Index

Meet the Author

David Petersen lives in the San Juan Mountains of south-western Colorado. For nearly 20 years, he has explored the western United States and writ-ten—for both children and adults —about many of its most interesting places and creatures. He has also written about Bryce Canyon National Park, Denali National Park and Preserve, and Death Valley National Park—all of these books are available from Children's Press.